phosphorus

phosphorus

HEIDI GARNETT

thistledown press

Library and Archives Canada Cataloguing in Publication

Garnett, Heidi, 1943-
Phosphorus / Heidi Garnett.

Poems.
Includes bibliographical references.
ISBN 1-897235-13-5

I. Title.

PS8613.A767P48 2006   C811'.6   C2006-903744-2

Cover artwork: *Little Remains* (gum-over-cyanotype) by Rajul Iyer
Book and cover design Jackie Forrie
Typeset by Thistledown Press
Printed in Canada

Thistledown Press Ltd.
633 Main Street
Saskatoon, Saskatchewan, S7H 0J8
www.thistledownpress.com

Thistledown Press gratefully acknowledges the financial assistance of the Canada Council for the Arts, the Saskatchewan Arts Board, and the Government of Canada through the Book Publishing Industry Development Program for its publishing program.

 Canadian Heritage

 Patrimoine canadien

 Canada Council for the Arts   Conseil des Arts du Canada

Acknowledgements

The author would like to thank *Event Magazine, Contemporary Verse 2, Carousel, The Dublin Quarterly, Quills, Ascent, Artistry of Life, Perigee*, the Ontario Poetry Society, the Canadian Federation of Poets and CBC radio for publishing and airing parts of this book. I would also like to thank the Banff Centre for the opportunity to work with Robert Hilles in the Wired Program who helped me put together the first manuscript, as well as Tim Lilburn, and provided space for me to work as an artist-in-residence. I can't thank the Banff Centre staff enough for their support and recognition. A special thank you to Patrick Lane, whom I had the opportunity to work with at Booming Ground and in an on-line program with five fellow poets. His challenging assignments raised the bar and changed the backbone of the manuscript.

I would like to express my deepest appreciation of John Lent and Mary Ellen Holland, professors at Okanagan College, who gave me the opportunity to join their classes and study with several amazing groups of students. Their writing encouraged me to explore new forms and subject matter. And, John and Mary Ellen's encouragement made all the difference, made me believe I could complete this manuscript. How fortunate I was that John Lent took a special interest in my work and acted as a mentor, opened doors into the world of writing. I can't thank him enough. And further to that, I must thank John again for his amazing work as my editor, his patience and kindness, his willingness to make changes and his wonderful critical eye, his intuitive sense of what works.

Thanks to my husband, Bob Garnett and my daughter Natasha who acted as ears, listened to me read countless poems. Thank you to my mother, Brunhilde Wiehler, for sharing her life so openly, even the most painful aspects of it, and my father, Horst Wiehler, deceased now, who was such a great story teller, my aunt, Magdalene Ziesemer, for her contribution. Without their stories this book would not be possible. I also wish to thank my dearest friend, Shirley Brayne, who has inspired me to choose again, to recreate my life.

And finally, many thanks to Thistledown Press for taking on this manuscript, for believing in the words.

CONTENTS

Those Who Are Gone But Don't Go

Small Atrocities

Ground Truth

In the Second Circle

Where Salt and Sweet Water Meet

For John Lent
Who makes writers of us all.

THOSE WHO ARE GONE
BUT DON'T GO

*Phos.pho.rus (symbol P) — a highly reactive,
poisonous element that ignites in air
and must be stored under water*

The ones we can't forget,
our skulls knitted together at the margins,
immovable, the articulations of bone and family,
eye orbits empty now, except for
ten small parts to build a home —
a roof, a floor, an inner and outer wall,
four angles, a circumference and
an apex[1] — a safe place,
a farm with a stove and food
several weeks walking distance
behind them. All gone,
fallen to earth, but they don't know it, or
believe it, don't know we left there
long ago. Even now, they can't rest,
their bones just below the surface.
They grope up through the permafrost,
are scattered by starved wolves.
We never heard from them, or
saw them again, never knew their burial place,
or if they escaped. That is our hope,
that they are living somewhere,
maybe India or Mongolia,
and have forgotten to tell us.

---

[1] The names of the bones around the eye

We find ourselves wondering
how it will feel to be doused
in gasoline, set on fire,
all of Berlin a bunker with windows
too small to fly through.
We find ourselves defending
the Pichelsdorf Bridges, sixteen
and under, no hope of living,
all of Berlin a playground, a zoo.
The zoo-keeper said men are fiercer
than gorillas. He stood beside
the dead female and wept, was known
to cry easily. The gods must have
averted their eyes, then, seen
how truly naked and ill equipped we were
to manage a world tipped on its axis.
They could have made us better,
given us faceted eyes, feathers,
hearts like dogs, even gills. But,
they were tired after making the plants
and animals, the sun, moon and stars.

Stalin will meet with Roosevelt and Churchill in Yalta
where it's warm in winter, make them fly
all that distance, though Roosevelt is dying,
and Stalin knows it. He wants to show them
Russia is more than the verb Siberia,
wants the world to believe Russia is a noun
stripped of its howl, quiet, civil, a city
beside a Black Sea. Roosevelt and Churchill
don't trust him. They know he writes words
in small books, changes their meanings,
ally to *enemy* and vice versa, whatever pleases him,
a wolf waiting for someone to drop behind.
They sign agreements, write foreign words.
Die Vershleppung[2], dragging away something
wild and dangerous, starvation tamed
to something acceptable, a verb to a noun.
The wolves in the Siberian woods have sickle eyes,
a thinness that keeps them awake at night.
They howl their restlessness at no one in particular.
All they know of agreements are trees marked
with the urine of an alpha male saying this is mine.
Now men have come to fell the trees.
Every day, men thin as bunk-bed slats
walk into the forest, pull saws between them,
breath freezing to beards. The trees fall
one after another, split the brittle silence
with sounds both beautiful and terrifying.

---

[2] The resettlement of all German nationals living in Russia in 1944 to Siberia. They were not allowed to leave a ten-kilometre radius, unless given permission, and survived by cutting trees. After ten years they were relocated again, many to Mongolia.

LINDEN TREES AT RAVENSBRUCK[3]

Pale yellow flowers squirm
from tasseled bracts, frayed ribbons
dangle between dark heart shaped leaves,
bouquets for women lying in beds
with small bone fragments
blossoming from their flesh.

I wonder does the pale bone,
the little ecru stranger
grafted into my numbered flesh
smell the steeped fermentation
of lemon and honey linden tea.
In our village they're called bee trees.

And the bees have come.

---

[3] A concentration camp outside of Berlin where bone fragment experiments
were performed on women

WE WALK ON BONE.

This land offers little comfort,
spreads itself wide and endless,
smells of salt and leaving.
We don't know who is buried
in our gardens, beneath the streets,
in the fields. The cows eat grass so green
you can't stand looking at it. Bones
claw up our of nowhere — a metacarpal
peeks through the strawberries, a tibia
stretches out in the tulips. Flowers
grow too beautiful, too large,
roses the size of dinner plates. At night,
irises exhale such perfume we close
the windows. Pewter lilacs
bristle like toilet brushes, flail
on arched canes, touch heads
to the ground in obeisance. We want
to do the same, but don't know how
to divide the blame.

The river originated high in the Beskidy Mountains,
flowed a thousand kilometres across the plains
past Krakow and Warsaw and Plock, gathering silt,
then depositing it where the river slowed and split
as it joined the sea. The alluvial delta,
half sunk below sea level, flooded every year.
People lived on small islands surrounded by
marsh water. If the island was substantial enough,
oak, beech and linden trees grew into copses,
the land became a small county. There were no roads.
People travelled the sluggish channels by boat.

Over the centuries, generations of farm sons
and the dispossessed built windmills,
dikes and dams, serviced them like lovers.
Guardhouses were built on top of the dikes,
farmers took turns watching day and night, when
the river ran high, settlers were warned with bonfires
when the river broke. Despite the danger,
people stayed. Eventually, the land dried,
the river straightened, the sea pushed back.
The land was rich, a vast triangle stretched between
the Vistula to the east and the Nogat to the west,
its base facing the Baltic, its heart
a free port called Danzig.

◦◦◦

She
Rarely spoke of the atrocities when captured
in East Prussia by front line troops in Spring, 1945.
Immigrated to Canada in 1950 with her husband and daughter.
Worked in restaurants and took in boarders.
Loved the water all her life.

Just before the water hurtles
two, three hundred feet
onto broken basalt columns,
shatters into new combinations
of blue and green, it pulls itself
back into a small cove,
a thin shiver clinging to its waiting,
a deep transparency,
a hold in the shifting below.

Fall 1944: There are no civilian monuments,
except the living testament of survivors.
There were no survivors in Nemmersdorf.
Everyone in the village murdered,
the only witnesses German soldiers
and photographs — women nailed to barn doors,
crucified you might say, girls and boys
on the ground, limbs bent like stork legs,
old men and women, heads half off.
The photographs might have been doctored.
Maybe Germans were the perpetrators.
The real atrocity still being debated
is the identities of the murderers.

The ice broken, the bridge gone and
you can't cross. There is nothing you can do
except wait, or go back. Scream,
much good it does you, like horses
breaking through March ice, pulled down
by wagons and people, photograph albums,

feather beds, giant waterlogged birds sinking.
Who knew horses could make such sounds.
The mind clattered like hooves on glass
when the river broke, almost followed the horses down.
Perhaps it's better to make a small sound,
a little click at the back of the throat, a switch
turning something off, a room you walk into,
sit on a hard-backed chair, feet flat, hands open.

The horse feels its way along the ruts, moves faster
now, ears pointed forwards, breath pluming.
It's eager to return to the others set free yesterday.
Herr Schultz speaks softly, slaps the reins
on the horse's back. He might as well be speaking
to the woman holding her baby. He doesn't
care much one way or the other if they cross the river.
He's old and tired, half frozen, not sure he wants to start
over again. The baby has been crying for hours,
no way to stop her, short of smothering.
Some mothers have already left small bundles behind.

For her there is only this decision to go back,
these wagons stretched miles ahead.
They wind between them. She holds her child,
wet to the belly, against her skin.
Her throat twists, makes sounds
she's never heard before. Tonight
they will be home. They will light the tile stove,
heat milk stirred with honey, look
from an upstairs window for other lights.
Herr Schultz will go to his own house,
maybe shoot himself, an absence of sound.
Everything waiting, artillery in the distance.
They will sleep together, a soundless sleep.
What comes tomorrow the heart will learn.

‑◦‑◦‑◦‑

Her Father
Died at age ninety in a nursing home in Canada,
a well-read man, a government bureaucrat.
Served in two World Wars. Only survivor of eleven boys.
Captured by the Russians at the end of WWII,
sent to Siberia but released, probably because of his age.
Worked as a dishwasher after he immigrated to Canada.
Stopped speaking the last seven years of his life.

‑◦‑◦‑◦‑

Speech becomes secondary
when you can't breathe.
You're sinking,
drowning in circumstances
beyond your control. You can't wave
with arms extended laterally, hands
flapping helplessly like broken wings.
In time, all movement stops,
legs become weights.
You sink vertically, like a bird
falling through the sky, too tired
to fly back to solid ground.

‑◦‑◦‑◦‑

All men aged thirteen to sixty-five
were sent into battle wearing armbands,
the *Volks Sturm*, the Civilian Storm —
tractors, threshing units lined roads,
ditches dug to slow the tanks. Men
singled out by SS, hung from telephone poles,
signs on their chests saying, *I am a deserter.*

Finally, the dikes were sprung, the rivers freed.
The land welcomed the water, reverted
to a shallow slough. Eels trailing death
slithered between brackish bushes; tilting trees
lifted branches upwards with such grace,
the birds fell silent, the bombing muffled.
A strange coherency hung over the still water
as people rowed away. If only they could
have grown scales and gills and swum to safety.

◦◦◦◦

My son, my dear son,
there you stand
in the foreground of
a sepia Velasquez painting,
the lapping darkness rising behind you.
I couldn't save you!
Filigrees of doubt fan
the edges of your lashed grey eyes,
too beautiful for a boy,
your stubbled hair
darkening from gold to brown
in the field of your perfect innocence.

Impossible leather boots,
how you hated them.
The narrow uniform
buttoned to your chin
strains to contain a boy
growing into man,
too soon. Behind you,
the Captain calls out the roll.
Time to go.

--o--o--o--

Her Mother
Dropped dead in the kitchen at age seventy.
Later discovered to be seventy-two,
had changed her age to immigrate to Canada.
Never saw a doctor, probably had a treatable heart condition.
Lost three of her four children, but never spoke about it.

--o--o--o--

ice creeps toward the centre
where it thins into memories
solid   but deceptive
fractured below the surface   with details
you don't want to know
don't go there
by the time you see cracks
fissuring from your feet
its already too late
you're standing on water and
the ice sinks beneath you   wait
until the heart freezes over
completely

--o--o--o--

Did I have four children once or
was that someone else?
I have a letter from my son's Captain
saying he was brave,
died without pain or complaint.
I don't believe him.
My son was too young and gentle,
I knew, even before he left,
I would never see him again.

And my girls, my beautiful girls,
one gone at thirteen months of diphtheria.
Sometimes, I feel a softness brush against
my breasts, and it reminds me
of her head lying there. The other,
betrayed by her womb, as we all are,
dead at age twenty-seven of a treatable
uterine infection, her casket
overflowing with red roses, a cortège
of horses and men. I thought death
could never touch me again,
the war over. I was punished
for my arrogance. They are buried
three different places, no one
visits them. I want to say their names,
to speak them aloud, to say,
You were never alone,
even when we ran away.
We carried you with us
through the snow.

·◇·◇·◇·

Uncle Herbert, Fritz and Gerhard, bachelor brothers,
arrested, *schlepped* to Siberia. We hear
they learned to lay ties and steel, to walk on snow
without breaking through, to keep hunger away
by chewing bark. They never came home.
A few did. They slipped through the forest
like shadows cast by the trees they felled,
imperceptible as minds unravelling,
found no one. No one they knew.
Some despaired then, stayed,
married Polish or Russian women,

made new lives for themselves, but
two or three walked further, found us.
My husband recognizable only
by the subtle intricacies of his movements.

◦◦◦

Her Husband
A merchant seaman, conscripted into the navy
when he returned to Germany from India.
Served on a submarine tender.
Sank three times, one of seven survivors in the North Sea.
Suffered from chronic heart problems due to exposure.
Rescued wife and baby daughter from East Prussia.
Loved gardening and found comfort there.

◦◦◦

At thirty feet you lose buoyancy,
sink like a stone. Everything slows, quiets
four miles below the surface. Hulls
buckle. Diaphanous jellyfish,
pale bottom feeders drift indifferently
above barnacled decks. Silted chairs, tables,
beds shift back and forth. No light,
no chance of reaching the surface again.
Seawater salts open wounds,
preserves them indefinitely.

◦◦◦

The torpedo explosion blows him skyward.
Looking down, he sees his cigarette
roll back and forth on the deck, the tip

still burning, his friend lying beside it,
dead, the ship hissing and gurgling,
sinking faster than his descent. Perhaps
the gods reached down and hung him
on the handle of the dipper, suspended him there.
Before the thought ends, he falls a hundred feet
within seconds. Debris swirls in circles,
follows the vortex down. He's unconscious
when pulled from the North Sea, hands
frozen onto a table, flashlight
clenched between his teeth, his heart
ruined. Doctors call it *Herzzersturrung*,
a disturbance of the heart.

Earth has been washed from his bones.
At night he dreams himself into a sea creature,
a flaccid thing swimming to the depths of a submarine;
searches for his lost comrades. And in daytime,
his feet hardly touch the ground, as he walks
about the farm, steps so lightly and silently
his wife fears he'll startle into flight and
disappear one morning. She tries to weigh him down,
root him in their life together,
but he is only air and water, unstable
elements not easily held or understood,
and finally, she lets him go.

◇·◇·◇

    The digging of memory:
    put the tip of the spade
    into the Spring soil. Push
    it in firmly with the right
    foot. Hold the spade steady,
    feel earth's gravity, how it takes

hold, wanting you to stay.
Earth is heavy, like the past,
doesn't want to let go.

The hoeing of pain:
In the early stages, it's
difficult to distinguish pain
from joy. They're both competing
for sun and space. If you
must differentiate, slice
weeds down with the sharp edge
of the hoe. Do it quickly,
thoroughly, so you
don't leave part of a root
to grow again.

The unearthing of graves:
In the fall, dig a narrow
trench, lay your memories in it.
Cover them with earth. Snow
and frost won't hurt them.
Later, when you're stronger,
use a pointed spade to cut
through the frozen surface
and find them bedded
underneath. The earth they
are buried in remembers them,
keeps them safe.

-◇-◇-◇-

Her Daughter
Although no conscious memory of the war,
suffered from severe nightmares until age thirteen.
Became a teacher, writer and family historian.

These stories, black and white photographs,
small pictures edged with pinking shears
in someone else's album. *Meine Tante*
perches on the lintel of our fireplace, left eye staring,
a gargoyle wearing a hearing aide. She
saw too much in Hamburg — a Rorschach of flames
five times taller than the Empire State Building,
people dancing jigs as they melted into asphalt,
their songs deafening. My other aunt
shows x-ray pictures of Dresden, a bone city
over exposed by a thousand bombers,
British by night, American by day.
She speaks in whispers, says
they are still occupied. These stories:
phosphorus. I try to keep my distance, but
they burn through flesh, can't be extinguished.

·○·○·○·

The third floor in St. Paul's Hospital,
my father tears tubes out and leaps again and again
against the windows in the intensive care unit
attempting to escape the cries of a woman
in the bed next to his. He thinks
he's leaping from his burning ship,
someone falling from an impossible height.

Alarm bells ring. Nurses run to restrain him
before he breaks the glass. He's sedated,
lifted into bed, tubes reinserted. The woman
continues to scream, *Help me, help me.*
He dreams his best friend stands at the foot of the bed.
His friend comes more often now,

looking as he did before he was burned.
That was my father's last escape attempt.

It's Christmas Eve. My father sits at the head
of the table, eyes closed, hands in his lap,
chin nodding into his chest. We're having his favourites,
goose stuffed with apples, potatoes and gravy,
jelly salad and red cabbage. A heaped plate
sits untouched in front of him. He says,
Everything can be taken from you,
except what you have learned.
Just keep talking, children, I'm listening.

He falls just a short distance, from the bed
to the bedroom floor, and says, *Oh*, eyes open.
Paramedics pump his chest, attach wires,
apply paddles, but he has left with his friend.
I stroke his thick white hair; feel life
bristling there and watch his face soften.

◦-◦-◦

The body eventually betrays us.
It carries traces of earth in its
large bones: the ulna, humerus, femur,
tibia and *os innominatum*, the nameless bones,
which bear no resemblance to any known object
and hold us upright in our pelvic bowls,
so we can see where we are going.

SMALL ATROCITIES

fos-for-us — (atomic number 15) —
a fundamental energy source in all living things,
the principal material in bones

Bones in a clearing, some dog tied to a tree,
the chain finally limp and forgiving, not a rope,
a chain, a guarantee, the vertebrae wandering.
Someone walked from the gravel road
cutting across the coulee. They walked
through the dry scrub, blow down poplars and
Saskatoon bushes along the Oldman River,
where no one will hear barking and digging.
Children find these places and say nothing.
They recognize bones and chains and
know to back away slowly,
know if they look too closely or touch,
disturb the desire for repentence,
something will get lost and never find home.
Atrocities require such a perfect innocence.

It wasn't the words we missed,
so much as the sound of them, their cadence,
lilt and rhythm, the lisping between the syllables,
our ancestors trying to explain something
before we leave on the *Beaverbrae*. Do you remember
that photo, your mother and you sitting on deck,
the poem underneath saying *Aufwiedersehen*,
the endless implications of a word translated
into *upon seeing you again*. We didn't believe it
and cried. A Canadian good-bye
more appropriate then. We paid
grave maintenance, planted hydrangeas,
never saw graveyards offering any comfort
on the prairies — wild overgrown places,
wooden falling-down crosses,
barely legible names, as if the dead are gone,
nothing to say. What a relief
to visit Germany eight years later.
No need to twist our mouths into sounds
we couldn't master, or pretend we understood
when we hadn't, to relax the ear.
The graveyards were beautiful. But soon,
we tired of conversations with the dead,
so many trying to speak at once, *der, die, das.*
We looked forward to returning.
Canada, its empty spaces prefaced
only by *the* and *a*, graveyards with room.
Sometimes, we spoke English without realizing it,
placed tongues correctly when saying s's and w's.

Some old animal memory tells me to find a den
when sun sets, pull blinds, curl up with others,
stay until light comes; an instinct,
that says it isn't safe to be alone in the dark;
maybe my mother told too many fairy tales,
the German versions with tragic endings.

Winter nights on the prairie,
I'd roll in my feather bed carried
from Bremerhaven, was wrapped in it
when we slept three high in the *Beaverbrae*,
on wooden benches in Colonial Cars
clacking from Quebec City to Lethbridge,
outside a slipping-by December,

cold and hard as lumps of coal;
a parting gift put in a child's shoe
set outside in November. It was night
when we arrived to strangers.
The coals still glowed on the coulees then,
bits of fire burning holes into the dark hills,
refusing to be extinguished.

My feather bed, the feel and smell of it, and
the flickering coal made long winter nights
bearable. I'd lie in bed and listen to snow
pelt against the window, think
how lucky I was to be warm and safe in Canada.
My mother often said, the worst part of the war
was the cold. I don't know

whether she was thinking about her brother
who died from a belly wound on the Russian front,
or her father captured in Konigsberg
taken to Siberia, or the time she tried to leave
by horse and buggy and turned back
because I was freezing in her arms.
Maybe, there are other stories,
ones she kept secret even from my father.

The town has almost disappeared.
Grain elevators rise and fall in the condensed heat,
jostle for solidity. Trains don't stop anymore.
They drag their lonely sounds behind them,
leave nothing for the townspeople to listen for.
Everything is becoming base, alkaline,
drifting like a dry summer snow, the sky
too wide and high, the sun too close,
the moon too low and orange.
The weight of abandonment pulls houses
into basements, fields into early fallow, stores
into closure. Everything is boarded up,
moving underneath, emptying and opening
unexpectedly. The town graveyard,
a picket crossword puzzle holding secret clues.
Cornflowers waver between the rows,

                    steal all the blue.

BEAN AND PEAR SOUP

When *chen* is added to your name
it's safe to take a chance,
say you were afraid today.
When my father called me *Heidchen*
I could tell him boys chased me home,
yelling DP, DP[4], that I'd cried,
they'd seen it. And he might say
it's okay, instead of saying,
Sticks and stones will break your bones,
but words will never hurt you. Even then,
I knew it was a lie. The power of *chen*
made it so. I'd sit on my father's lap,
watch my mother cook bean and pear soup,
smoked pork ribs, the last beans,
potatoes, Anjou pears picked green
in Kelowna, stacked under our feet in
the back seat of the Chevy. The pears
not touching in a dresser drawer,
off limits except to check for ripeness,
each ingredient in a certain order,
sweet and salt respectful of each other.

---

[4] Displaced Person

1.

Out on the prairie,
things become clearer, trees thin,
the sky rises to great depths,
a two hundred mile blue sinkhole,
the land stretches itself, silts the bottom.
Each blade of grass sways gently.
We see through air like water,
each small thing magnified, made precious.

> You could spend hours
> looking at the Sears Roebuck catalogue
> fatter than a dictionary, plenty of wishes.
> Imagine yourself in that dress — red
> strawberries sprinkled on white eyelet cotton,
> skinny red plastic belt, red buttons marching
> down the front of a perfect five foot two.
> God, you'd look just like her,
> if you could afford it. Later,
> when the catalogue was out of season,
> you'd cut those dresses out with tabs,
> play cut-out-dolls,   even though you were ten,
> and expected to baby sit.

2.

December, 1950,
arrived in Lethbridge, Alberta,
coals burning on the hills.

> Snowflakes fall continually
> landing on the thin edge of day,
> sharp branches and stems break,
> a din of crystal fractures.

Sailed from Bremerhaven, Germany,
ten days on a leaking converted freighter,
women segregated from men
across a sea-sick ocean. In Quebec City
received ten dollars per person and
a care parcel with Noxzema cream in it,
bought Ukrainian sausage and rye bread
in Winnipeg from women dressed like bears,
three days sitting up on wooden benches
wrapped in feather beds.

3.

The local farmwomen threw a welcome shindig.
My father in a navy double-breasted suit, my mother
a rabbit fur coat and black velvet hat and gloves.
(Always look your best.) Menu: turkey with stuffing,
mashed potatoes, creamed corn, mixed peas and carrots,
jelly salad and apple pie. Familiar foods: potatoes, peas, carrots.
(My father said corn is pig food, and he wasn't going to eat it.)
Gifts: homemade-strawberry-jam, crab apple jelly,
sack of russet potatoes, sack of winter onions, leg of ham,
knitted socks, mittens, toques, three grey woolen blankets and
an entire set of yellow melamine dishes for eight from Sears.
My mother cried. We were ready to set up house in two rooms
above Thaell's Tailor Store and Men's Haberdashery.

4.

On August afternoons, when it's too hot
to continue threshing, farm women
pressing crabapples into jelly
leave boiled lids and jars to cool,
make their way upstairs to bedrooms,
oval rag rugs on waxed linoleum floors,

drawn oilskin blinds. Naked men with
sun-burned necks stand in half-light
privates pulled up into chapped hands
crossed shyly. The comfort waiting there,
the sweet scent of pressed apples.

5.

Fort Macleod, a two-beer parlour town
strung along the Old Man River, nips
at the knees of the Porcupine Hills and
stumbles toward the Rockies. Blackfoot,
disguised in wolf skins and buffalo calf skins,
once called to buffalo at Head-Smashed-In-Buffalo-Jump.
Called, not chased, called out of respect
for their kinship with all living things,
the meat divided according to need.

> *The people and the buffalo make a circle*
> *as they pass together across the plains,*
> *and the six seasons and the thirteen moons*
> *come again and again.*

But who knew about First Nation's people.
Once a year, in the Whoop-up Days Parade,
we saw Blackfoot, as they used to be,
women and children dressed in buckskin
sitting on hay bales stacked on flatbeds,
painted warriors riding unshod horses,
dancing beaded and belled birds, drummers.
Our eyes followed them down the street.

6.

It was the horses,
the dappled horses
galloping away from lariats,
saddles, bits and bridles,
tails and manes furling.
We followed them
through the chattering grass,
prancing, slapping our sides,
tossing shorn heads,
neighing, jostling one another,
as if we belonged to that herd.
When they were out of sight,
we pressed our ears to the ground,
listened to the thrumming of hooves,
the passing of our youth.

7.

I went to school in March,
almost eight in grade one,
in June, promoted to grade two
unable to read or write English.
I learned to dream with eyes open,
traded pigtails for bobs and bangs,
hand knitted dresses for pants, plaid roll-ups.
Dad worked as a baker, mom a short order cook/waitress
at the Palomino Café/Bakery.

8.

Along highway three, just after you leave town,
you'll see Pearl's place, hunkered down behind
the billboard for the Palomino Café/Bakery —
a rearing golden horse, flaxen mane and tail,

tears at the sky with slashing hooves.
Pearl befriended me, the weird DP[5] kid,
and I was glad to have a friend, even if she
used catalogue pages for toilet paper,
lived by the tracks and had older brothers,
bigger and scarier than a Blackfoot.
We spent hours, *hours* looking at the Sears
catalogue, especially men's underwear.

9.

Pearl's place,
a bend-kneed raw plank shack,
its low
       sloping
              roof crouched into a thin cleft.

This is where fences and sidewalks
hang onto the backend of town,
lean away from the symmetry of some other creator
imagining one hundred and fifty grasses:

                    beak grass
                    fox sedge
                    purple love grass
                    silky wild rye
                    fringed brome
                    big bluestem and Indian grass
                              taller than men

and further down slope
              at the edge of wetter ground
                              prairie cord grass
                                  also known as rip gut
finely serrated leaves like knives.

---

[5] Displaced Person

And this is where clocks fold their hands and
stop to watch flowers lever origami selves
out of a tangle of bulbs, corms and rootstalks,
                             seven feet deep,
the slow processional of sun and moon,
their pathways strewn with colour:

                    purple and blue-
                             violets
                             shooting stars
                             cone flower
                             bachelor's buttons

            pink-

                             Alberta wild rose
                             toadflax
                             foxglove-beard tongue
                             prickly pear cactus

            yellow and white-
                             pussy toes
                             prairie parsley
                             black-eyed Susan
                             dandelion

In November,
when the land begins its long sleep and
your breath is squeezed to zero by the wind
tobogganing down Big Chief Mountain, the house
disappears beneath crusted snow waves,
            except for
a thin smoke signal roping upwards
in search of some other sky.

10.

Second Christmas,
ordered almost every type of candy
from the back of the Sears *Wish Book.*
(My father said we'd starved enough and,
were going to eat whatever we damn well wanted.)

      chocolate Santas
      jaw breakers
      sugar babies
      wax lips
      humbugs
      mallo cups
      candy ribbon, and
                  best of all,
      candy cigarettes

Dad got Players tobacco
loose in the can.
He smoked
hand rolled,
long Zigzag sleeves
squeezed and licked,
razored into threes.

I got a mail order farm,
red metal barn, white plastic fences,
one brown horse, two Hereford cows, a flock
of white chickens, one rooster, some ducks,
two sheep and three pink pigs, the best gift
ever. In the evening, we look at pictures.

11.

My father, the oldest, sits sideways
legs crossed, hair parted sharply,

a Victorian chair. He wears his one suit,
white shirt, tie knotted casually in the French manner.
His brother Rudolf, killed at Stalingrad,
wears an imitation sailor suit, fashionable
for pubescent boys. He stands to the side,
already leaving, his face so open, you'd think
he was someone's special child. Their sister,
in danger of dying from a heart defect,
wears a white blouse, black bolero jacket.
She balances precariously on the chair's arm..

12.

Pearl and I lie among the millennial flowers,
arms crossed on our chests.
Clouds shape themselves into
thrashing stallions. The prairie
laps against the bow of our heads.
We sleep on homemade bunk-beds,
her parents and brothers at the American Hotel.
Small creatures swim beneath our pillows,
whisper with grass voices.

13.

In the beginning all the world was water. One day, the Old
Man, also called Napi, was curious to find out what might be
beneath the water. He sent animals to dive beneath the
surface. First duck, then otter, then badger dove in vain. The
Old Man sent Muskrat diving to the depths. After a long
time, muskrat rose to the surface holding between his paws a
little ball of mud and blew upon it. The mud began to swell,
growing larger and larger until it became the whole earth.
The Old Man then made the people.
(Head Smashed In Buffalo Jump UNESCO site)

14.

The other day, we were talking
about what frightens us, and
I said the past. You can't change it.
It's always hanging behind you,
like a tail on a dog. You can run
as fast as you want, but
when you stop, there it is,
hanging off your rear end,
wagging at you. That's when
I want to fall on my knees and
ask forgiveness for something.

15.

I wanted a blue single speed CCM bike badly:

> page 363 Sears *Spring/Summer*
> baked on enamel finish
> positive-stop coaster brakes for fast/secure stops
> fully reflectorized for safe night riding
> miles of riding fun

I was going to get it,
if I didn't see Pearl anymore.
(We were coming up in the world.)
We had a three-bedroom crushed green
stucco house and three-dimensional
realistic-interior Laurentian brick
on the kitchen walls, a console record player/radio
on which we listened to *The Lone Ranger,*
a fenced yard and sidewalks running
along both sides of the street, a baby brother
and kids willing to play with me.
(Never let them see you're hurting.)

16.

if
I put my fingers
                    like scissors
in the air between us and
snip the rope frayed
thin as a string
or
turn the curved ear of my rudder away
from the warm cove of your friendship
or
loosen the rusted nail
                    grown to flesh
pinning my thigh to yours
perhaps
my narrow keeled boat
                    a fragile thing held
                    together with ribs and skin
will capture singing birds in
its floundering wind cloth and
follow the secret drift of grass and
the little iron fish
                    pointed to true north
floating
in the bowl of my heart

17.

I never saw Pearl again.
We moved a year later.
My father got a better job,
my mother took in six boarders
to make the house payment.
I did dishes for ten, went to class,

read *True Romance* magazines,
became a naturalized Canadian.

18.

Give me the long road unraveling over the land,
a raffia ribbon running to the thin lip of the horizon.

Recently, I drove through Ft. Macleod
en route to Lethbridge to visit family,
turned left onto the dusty road
along the tracks, the house still there:

>sliver grey
>>abandoned
>blue and white sky
>outlined on the blank floor
>a sea of wild barley
>laps against the foundation
>wavering in one hundred ten degrees
>pigeons in the attic
>>cool cooing
>grey dust feathers
>drift across the boards
>chewed by mice
>>small hurryings
>the smell of wind spice
>>alfalfa
>>hay and wild roses
>blonde summer girls
>banging screen door boys
>windows flash
>broken glass

GROUND TRUTH

Phosphorus has multiple forms
in the same physical state

If I was accustomed to being alone,
I would learn a hundred names for snow,
      abrasive as sand in wind.
I would know fresh snow is a breathing
ice skeleton that can reinvent itself as
      spring snow
      sugar snow
      kinetic snow
          because
snow that lasts more than a year,
can harden into firn
on its way to becoming glacial.

A pure deep snow
      high as knees
surrounds our home,
indigo honeycombs,
      thirty below.
The porch door bangs open, and
I jump up, thinking you've come
your breath disappearing behind you,
but no one's there.

Today heavy snow
dragged me to the ground.
Hexagonal crystals froze my throat closed with
symmetrical branches and stems,
      so wildly beautiful,
I wondered why five or seven
might not do as well.

It's winter in Clyde River.
The northern lights are tissue paper
folded into greens and mauves and blues.
Stars outnumber man's imagination and curve
under the weight of light speeding outwards
in a universe with no edges or center.
The frozen ocean is indistinguishable from land.
Three hours a day, the sun pulls itself weakly
above the horizon, glows like a rose boudoir lamp,
then collapses back behind the shadow of the world.
Soon day will merge into night and disappear completely.
Land and water and sky lose their edges in the dark,
until you can't tell one from the other. And sometimes,
you feel like you're swimming in stars,
pushing them ahead of you.

An Arctic wind blowing sideways
across the tundra can lift an Inuit man
with his arms stretched out flat
and standing on his tiptoes
so the earth doesn't pull him back.
And he can see all his comings and goings
and speak bird sounds he's never heard as
he dreams himself into snowy owl or raven.
He can see winter coming early, its dark teeth
chewing at the underbelly of day
pulling it down, like prey. He sees light snow
begin to fall softly in still air, *qanniapualuk*,
collecting on branches, *qali*. How
light snow can break a tree in half.
How ptarmigan change from brown to white,
their feathers soft ripple marks in the snow, *tumarinyiq*,
and how foxes grow silver coats.
How life can fly at you, a blizzard of ice needles,
unless you know where to find
wind-hardened snow cover, *upsik*,
and the *inuksuks*[6] you built in the summer.

---

[6] A construction of rocks piled on top of one another used as location and welcome markers, but also having other significance.

Snow evolves,
a semi-infinite matrix,
      ice grains
      air and water
      dust and pollen
an ecosystem supporting colonies,
      bacteria
      algae and
      snow worms
the smell of fresh watermelon.

Our cabin over the roof in snow.
We've tunneled through our hiatus
to the surface, winter moles,
contracted eyes squinting
against a scaffolded snowpack,
throwing back blue refraction.
It breathes. Today
we drill cores
two hundred feet deep.

The core —
concentrations of oxygen isotopes,
slices of dark and light,
summer and winter,
wind-tumbled time
compressed into something immeasurable,
no two alike,
a remote sensing
blown through in drifts.
Who can truly verify
the permutations and
combinations of separation?

The snowpack looks safe today, solid and old,
no rollovers, wind-loaded areas , shaded aspects,
no evidence of young faceted snow, but it can
fool you, slide away from the weight of one skier.
I've checked alpha angles, fracture lines,
run out distance. The weather report sounds good,
no recent avalanche activity, whumping noises
shooting cracks, even so, I hammer the snow,
ski test a couple of small slopes.

I choose a line off to the edge,
instead of centre punching, so I can jump
to the side, if the slope cuts loose. I've ridden
the dragon, know he likes the straight line
down the middle. The straight line,
I always skied it. Hell, I was invincible,
nothing could touch me.

We didn't carry beacons, wear safety straps
on skis and poles. We carved the new snow
like it had been laid down for us alone,
two lines intersecting in a serpentine braid,
white marble with blue veins.
Have you ever seen Michelangelo's *David*?
It was like that. You could see every vein,
every curve of pale flesh, feel it pulsing,
although it was cold, cold as stone.

Jim's hand looked that way.
It stuck out of the snow like it belonged there,
a disembodied hand reaching for a beautiful sky.
The roar of the avalanche now the sheered edge
of a silence I never want to hear again.
I was carried down slope, out of control,

clinging to the back of a howling dragon.
He rolled me into his coils, buried me
under ten feet, or so. I was lucky.
My hands instinctively protected my face,
created an air space. I could breathe.

I drew in air and screamed.
I screamed and was glad for it. We were alone.
I'd never felt an alone like that, although now
it comes on me, even when I'm in a crowd.
I didn't know whether I was head up or down,
but knew to let spittle run from my mouth;
it ran down. I dug, my hands metal tools,
my mind a machine. I dug my friend out.

His mouth full of snow, eyes open,
face like marble, veined white marble.
I just sat there rocking Jim, rocking myself.
We sat that way through the night, me
rocking us and talking. The next day, a rescue party,
and that's pretty well the end of the story.
I ski alone now — an old fool.   Sometimes,
I feel cold breath blowing off the cornices,
watch it curl into tongues lapping at my knees.

I don't think I know her, but
if I did, she's changed
                secretively
in some towered room with
a slitted window where you can see
the true trajectory of the world,
if you press your eye against the opening.

The small mortared cell
contains a single iron bed
covered with a hand-stitched quilt:
                            Tree of Life, not
                            Oak Leaf and Reel, or
                            Grandmother's Flower Garden,
but, Tree of Life
stitched seven to the inch
by Amish women living halfway
between Eden and Paradise.
The feathered branches hang
with red pendulous fruit and writhe
across a seamless sheet of white cotton,
sewn in close parallel lines.

Beside the bed, a shaker chair
worn into plainness, and
on the back of the five stride wall
a calendar with pictures of trees:
                            trees with blossoms, or
                            red and green leaves, except for
                            November through March
when icicles stab
at a black and white sky, and
fear jams its thumb
into the clear eye of remembrance.

The last time I saw her
she said, *I should let you go,*
rather than hold you
with the weight of my love, but
tonight we will drink green tea,
spiced with mango and peach,
from these cups whose bellies
have been warmed by my hands.

It had many aspects,
this work healing the psyche.
Quiet weeping, a seated circle, an intangible shape.
We were afraid to look at each other,

admit anything. The lake
outside the window. Sound of music playing,
people launching boats, laughing,
hours passing, days

like years. The language of despair;
always changing, yet the same, something Jungian
we could get our teeth into, tear at.
How so and so hurt us

badly, damaged our egos; a frail omnipotence
we constructed long ago, safeguarded
by blame and excuses. We watched
sails swamp in the wind and

fell into each other's arms, wept openly. The sun,
finally. And God:
we thought He had forgotten us,
felt responsible.

I can't remember how to breathe.
I've forgotten almost everything,
except your hands cupping my breasts.
They fit perfectly.
Your mouth decorates my throat with necklaces,
my body collects itself beneath yours.
You speak a language I only understand in dreams,
sounds I've never heard before.
I answer back with a language of my own,
drift somewhere just above drowning.
Breathing is an act of grace.

There are things we'd rather not think about:
the gnarled sticks of autumn, bare pear branches
etched on a sharp blue longing, the forgiveness of leaves
fallen, fruit, the geese feeding in the orchard,
lifting as one, feet straggling behind them.
They think of nothing but returning south,
call and call with their long hollow throats,
but we don't listen, don't want to watch that leaving.
We learned long ago some voices are better not heard.
We welcome the white bones of winter conversations,
the tiny requests of sparrows, the silence of snow,
watch it settle, wrap ourselves in it. The morning cold
tries to nip us awake, but we stay to the wooden fences,
the baffle of drifts collected there, and listen
to the sounds of our footsteps and the dog
running ahead of us, barking, barking.

my electric hair
eddies across your bare chest
we drive
    half naked
    windows down
through the night
to avoid one hundred ten degrees
the desert breathes
stillness in motion
red rock contracts and
cracks open

saguaro cactus
        clearly visible
stand two centuries
ladder backed and dreaming
ranks of grizzled giants
drilled through by gila woodpeckers
and northern flickers
elf owls *hoo hoo*
    softly

we stick to the road
your new two-door hardtop
sit close
swear we'll always sit this way
your left hand on the wheel
the other on my knee

The path is a bevelled margin falling off
into the milky limestone wash of Green River.
Straggly dogwoods, already past their bloom in
mid June, cut-work cedars and deeply chiseled
evergreens throw gnarled roots, like ropes,
across the path, but some tilt precariously
in an awkward *pas de deux* with another.
We've been warned to watch where we step,
be careful of the rare brown boa snake,
often mistaken for a large earth worm, but
all we see is millipedes — glistening black
two fluorescent orange stripes
running down their backs, little railroad tracks
hurrying to smooth destinations.
The upper lookout is above the drop.
Foaming water and pebbles pestle
the humped rock into potholes or bridges.
The lower lookout overlooks the fall
squeezing and gurgling through constricted rocks
that battle to keep control. On a small island
two ancient cedar trees worn almost to ladders,
support one another with spindly fringed arms.
Their roots crawl over rocks for a foothold.
On the way back, we hang onto the frayed edge
of the path, watch our feet carefully.

He was about forty, handsome
even in death, the skin waxy,
yellowed by formaldehyde. Lines
curved from the mouth and nose to the chin,
furrowed straight across the forehead, places
where he had clenched his face repeatedly.
After class, we named him Waldo, laughed
about finding him. We needed
that distance, wanted reassurances
we were more than flesh
draped over two hundred bones, although
we couldn't verbalize it then.
He was ours to dissect for two semesters.

We were relieved to crack his ribs open
with medieval looking instruments, his face
covered by a sheet. We let him sleep
while we removed his heart,
laid it on the dissection table, as if
it could speak, reveal its secrets,
tell us its history. We cut it open
searching for the mouths of small veins, semi-lunar valves,
the columns of Carneoe, pillars
holding the heart upright, foreign places
we'd read about, the knowledge we needed. At night,
we dreamt about Lazarus.

Months later, when his torso
lay exposed to the backbone, we realized
we'd never find him, no matter
how carefully we drew pictures of lungs and livers and hearts,
named parts, analyzed them. We grieved,
without knowing it, felt older,
tired. We stopped joking,
sewed him back together, sent him home
to be buried, saw
the first faint tracings of lines around our eyes,
when we looked at each other closely.

Rhonda sits at the edge of two cliffs jutting above Costa del Sol. White plastered houses wind down narrow cobbled streets toward the bullring. Hemingway came here to watch the great ones fight, as did Orson Wells, among others. Photos of them hang in the museum beneath the bleachers, silk matador suits in glass cases, fuchsia pink, turquoise and peach, men's colours in the ring, and the mounted heads of many bulls, their glass eyes gazing toward the dry mountains. Today, the bullring is silent, its edges draped in red and gold velvet, six large wreaths slashed with satin banners wilt on metal stands, the funeral service done. A latecomer weeps and lays an open letter at the feet of a bronze statue, a matador piled to the knees with red roses. Antonio Ordonez, the son of Nino de Palma, has died of lung cancer, the inspiration for the handsome young bullfighter in *The Sun Also Rises*, his ashes strewn in the ring, home again. Embroidered with a thousand lights, he twisted and twirled his lithe body into a sword hidden beneath a cape, and drove himself deep into the beating heart of the bull, before he was impaled. This is what we admire about him. He waited for the horns, without stepping aside or flinching.

IN THE SECOND CIRCLE

Phosphorus (specific gravity 1.82)
exists in kinetic and thermodynamic forms,
one known as alpha, the other beta.

We first saw the lovers
on the ceiling of The Opera in Paris,
Chagall's euphoric faces
floating above us. We stood
in the second circle, heads thrown back,
eyes shaded to appreciate
irrelevance; our relationship
hardened into *bas relief*, plaster *tromp de l'oeil*,
red and gold, roles defined so long ago
we'd forgotten the reason. That week
an assassination attempt on Jacques Chirac,
some disgruntled lover with a gun
wrestled to the ground by a Canadian tourist.

When awarded the Medal of Honour,
he said bravery isn't a conscious choice.
It's a spontaneous act,
an instinct, like breathing.

Not far from Cannes
we happen upon Chagall's burial place,
a small graveyard with a view,
an unobtrusive hillside town,
hardly noticed by tourists.

They say it's the light
draws people to the Riviera
keeps them there, that eternal quality
seen when we shade our eyes
look beyond the second circle.

OTHER PEOPLE
(*for Corrie*)

So we talked
how your mother heard
her handicapped child died
of pneumonia, how my father stole
me from the hospital when I was ill,
how your father was imprisoned
for saying Germany might lose
the war, how my grandfather was
the chauffer for the camp Commandant;
how your uncle walked
to Siberia, how my uncle was
castrated, how my parents buried
your grandparents, said
the service. The conversation
earlier was about other people;
people with cleaning ladies,
hairdressers; people who have
pedicures, lunch with friends;
people who believe
in fridges, washing machines,
king-sized beds, light switches, stores
with groceries, banks that open.
They believe
there will be heat
when they want it, magazines and
candy, facial cream, underwear.
They believe
the world will continue
as it is. We watch
them closely, copy them.

FOG

Some things aren't negotiable.
Look how fog moves
like a sleepwalker in bare feet,
how it brushes
against trees and bushes, memorizes
low places, as if it wants
to settle. See
how it thins into fingers
when the sun rises, a vague resolve
to touch, to remember. How impossible
to remember your father this way,
aqueous and grey as his eyes,
still looking, solid and immoveable
as a stopped heart, the floor
beneath him; how
you don't grieve enough
to stop him from leaving;
breathing just a reflex
you can't control, the importance
of a doorjamb, something wooden,
when you cling to what was.

An incredible memory for detail,
decisive in the O.R., but
prone to take chances, wing it
on her own. You can't make me do it, and
if you try, I likely won't.
Some protective mechanism
shut down in childhood
before she could logic her way through it,
maybe an overbearing mother, but
it's never that simple. Perhaps
an insanity we all suffer from.
Despite advice from friends and counselling,
she stayed in a relationship
that became more and more abusive.
I use the word abusive
without fully understanding it, because
she contributed to it as much as he,
had the means to leave. In fact,
she did, but always went back,
as if she rejected the whole notion
of death as a diagnosis, a surgeon's arrogance,
or maybe, she knew exactly
what she was doing.

Who knows why we chase boys with drugs,
drift into the headlights of oncoming traffic,
mesmerized; a vague disappointment
when we crank the wheel away
from putting a gun to our heads, or
swallowing a bottle of pills. I tried
to talk to her many times, but
she didn't hear anyone's voice;

only his. They were gorgeous together.
At the winter ball she'd dress
in something clingy, cut on the bias,
hair pulled straight back and
twisted into a French roll, he
tailor-made, handsome. She never drank,
said she was the designated driver.
The frustration knowing
it would end badly.
She had it in her head
she could heal him, or
heal herself, six generations
forward and back. Each time
he hurt her, he'd cry like a baby,
promise never to do it again, classic.
When I got the news she'd been murdered
I wasn't surprised, deeply affected,
but not surprised. Those of us who knew her
had been waiting, holding our breath
as we watched her step closer and
closer to the edge, taking off one restraint
after another, dropping them
like soiled scrubs, until she stood there naked,
perfectly naked. My God, she was beautiful.

The coyotes lived in the apple orchard all summer.
I'd see them when I walked, two thin intruders
watching, ears pricked, heads turning as
their eyes followed me casually.
I resented their slitted stares,
their narrow muzzles poking at me,
forcing me to brush against
Oregon Grape and prickly blackberries
tangled in the fences. I thought, *They're a danger.*
I'm going to report them to the authorities,
have them removed by Conservation Officers. —
knowing it meant they'd be shot. After all,
this orchard was in the middle of a city,
not bordering a forest.
I wondered how they'd found their way here,
how their thinness had served them
as they slipped past cars and people,
like ground fog, half there.

That was the year you were arrested, our lives
dissected. I could hardly leave the house
except to walk in the orchard, afraid
someone would recognize me, ask questions
I couldn't answer. I wanted to hide,
crawl into a burrow,
a tight safe place no one would find,
a place to cry and poultice my wounds
with cool dark earth. I was ashamed to be so visible,
so dependent on the good opinion of others.
The coyotes never sought my approval, nor

resented my presence. They simply
lived their lives, cautious,
reliant on no one but each other. In time,
I learned to sit on a log near the fence,
quiet, watching,
and they'd sit on their mound
measuring the distance between us
with yellow eyes.

She knew.
She knew even before they swarmed her —
stinging words settling one by one,
each with its own whispering voice,
encasing her in their conversations until she heard
only one long protracted vowel and felt nothing,
except the tiny honeyed feet
sealing her lips and eyes with waxy hexagons of silence.

She had known long ago,
but said nothing,
believing words are too small, too fragile,
to encompass such emptiness.
    Death —
she would blow the word out again and again
in the buzzing hive of her dreams —
gauzy bubbles impaling themselves
on the teeth of the distant horizon, and then,
awaken to find her cold fingers
tracing the edges of the scar lying across her chest —
a thin crescent slivered from a winter moon.

Where to now?
Bedside vigils and reconciliations abandoned years ago,
the quiet hush of muffled rooms?
Or, finally,
simply, gratefully,
speaking in metaphor,
phrases fanning out,
a gossamer humming.

He can still hear his wife when he doesn't speak,
the insistence of her slippers pattering down the hall,
the door opening, her kiss, the hiss of her taffeta robe
as she bends over him,
a gift. Their granddaughter chose it
because it said, *listen, listen,* when it moved.
She never felt listened to, never understood
you don't have to speak to be heard,
never learned the comfort of silence.
He gets up at nine, reads in his room
until lunchtime, eats his sandwich and jello,
sits in the vinyl chair by reception one to three,
naps until five, eats again, watches TV;
slices the days into twos, each segment
a contract. He listens to nurses talk,
patients complain. He doesn't want to hear
anymore; his children ask how long he plans to live,
although they don't say it
aloud. He asks himself the same question
every two hours, rages silently at gods
who break agreements. It's been ten years
since his wife dropped dead in the kitchen,
seven years since he spoke. Tonight,
he will take another vow of silence,
lay in bed, strain to hear the whisper of taffeta.

BONZAI

Bind my feet and I'll live forever
pruned into a small intangibility.
The secret of perpetual old age
is in the constriction of feet and
strangulation of the heart.

STRAIGHT UP

I stand at the bottom of my grief.
It stretches straight up
with no hand or footholds to guide me,
no light. I look for the moon and stars
and can't find them, can't see
how I will ever climb that rock face,
I'd need to grow wings
and fly above it,
become something living.

WHERE SALT
AND SWEET WATER MEET

*Phosphorus from the Greek word "phosphoros"
meaning bearer of light*

My mother said,
I wanted to kill myself,
but couldn't. We saved each other
when I was three and continue to.
She's eighty and I'm sixty
and still in need of saving.
We're still trying to learn the lesson
of tenderness. Even now,
years distant from a soldier
putting a knife in her belly,
my mother isn't certain
it's safe to gentle herself
too much. She might break
completely then, never find her way
back to Canada. Today,
we're at our favourite beach.
It's rocky, not nearly as beautiful
as the *Frische Haft*, where salt
and sweet water meet. She complains
her hips hurt, her shoes don't fit,
she can't bend over. I get on my knees,
pull her beach shoes on
see how thin her legs have become,
the skin skimmed milk
poured over bones, her feet
birds' feet turned inwards
clinging to their one branch.

If Gods Watched

It was my father's faith that saved him,
the determination of a man clinging
to the definition of himself as saved.
He told the story of his rescue repeatedly,
never took the credit he deserved.
He would say he couldn't have clung
to the ship's debris without God
by his side. I say anything is possible
if you hold on long enough.
I have no questions for my father.
But, God has a great deal to answer for.
He left us with a reminder of His doubt,
touched our hearts with His icy finger,
as we floated unconscious, pulled
the twisted columns of Carnaoe[7] down.

---

[7] Columns holding up the chambers of the heart

LOVERS

I see them more and more as I get older.
They have a certain look about them,
as if they know something, a secret
they told each other while making love.
Their bodies dusted with silk powder,
ask to be touched. They
drop flowers behind them, violets or
periwinkle from the sheets they slept on,
leave beds unmade, dishes
on the nightstand. Hair
always half wet, faces washed,
clothes clean, but wrinkled. They
talk with their eyes, ask for everything.
And when one dies, a surety
settles on the other — a knowledge
they were beautiful once,
immortalized.

BAOBAB TREES

The old ones are hollow,
as most old things are,
the rings on their narrow rinds
barely legible. No one truly
knows their age. Here,
at the edge of the great Kalahari,
they grow fat on pink sand.
Tentacles wave dark green leaves
shaped like human hands.

PENTIMENTO

Something changed.
Love became a resistance,
thin layers of grievances
painted between us. Now,
an underlying image shows through
more and more each day, the surface
yellowed and transparent with age,
a familiarity not entirely solid,
a kind of hope.

PURPLE IRISES

Did Paul's vision diminish gradually,
without his knowing, a small seed
growing slowly into a purple iris with a yellow throat.
It's loveliness driving him down a shaft so deep,
the sky retreated to a point above him,
a needle of light pinning him like a butterfly,
his flutters dusting the ground, finally ceasing.
Or was it a sudden luminous experience
as he looked directly into the light, unable to speak
or turn away from the beauty of purple irises
blooming in his eyes, blinding him.
He was led into Damascus like a child.

If Death Called

If death called,
said he was coming for a visit
would I say my brother and
his wife are coming and
we have no room,
the climate wouldn't agree
with him, our house is difficult
to find and I'm feeling fine —
physically — but not well enough
to be a hostess, that at any moment,
I might begin to scream,
beat on the walls with my fists
for their damnable complacency,
lock myself in the closet and
stand among yesterday's coats
and shoes, run off into the woods,
tear at the stoical trees
until my hands bleed and
birds go mad with my weeping,
or would I say, Come,
let us sit together, sip
a cup of tea and say nothing,
for there is nothing left to say.

PORCHES

dusk drifts
over the living room floor
light gone to seed
we walk through it
from the kitchen
to the porch
scatter it with our bare feet
it rolls back
so softly and quietly
we don't notice it
fill the empty spaces
behind us
evening wraps us
in its shawl
settles on our shoulders

If I lay on the night bed
beneath a star-studded coverlet, my head
resting on a pillow embroidered with moons
circling through their phases,
would my shoulders and hips align with stars
like a constellation, one eye
a red dwarf, the other a white giant, my hair
a nebulae, a spill of light
seeping into darkness, my arms and legs
mythical, my mouth a black hole
singing Vedas. Or, would my body
align with gas and dust, become the sound
of a copper temple bowl tapped
with a wooden mallet, notes
circling ever outwards, a faint glow
in every direction.

SLOW JAZZ IN WATERTON
(for Bob)

What kept me coming back,
was that slow jazz you played.
Sarah Vaughn singing, *Embrace me,*
you sweet embraceable you,
at 33 rotations per minute.
Your small upstairs room,
single bed, black and white television set,
bureau, straight backed chair,
a narrow window overlooking Main Street,
deer eating geraniums at 2:00 a.m.
and another couple, strangers
sitting in the stairwell
outside your door, listening.
Sarah singing, *Embrace me,*
you irreplaceable, you.

ALMOST EIGHTY-EIGHT
(for M.Z)

I hadn't seen *meine kleine Tante,*
my little aunt, my second mother,
for over a year. She had celebrated
her life three times, the same Wiener schnitzel
dinner in the German Club, accompanied by a
good Rheinhessen wine, apple strudel for dessert,
followed by late night sandwiches — sausage
and cheese on thinly sliced rye — and speeches
and songs. She never expected to live this long.
She was first to survive open-heart surgery in Europe,
second in the world, her chest a roadmap
only surgeons could read. When she immigrated to Saskatoon,
doctors at the university shook her hand. And, her back,
a foreign landscape of shrapnel burrows and jumbled sticks.
My hand leapt away when she put it there, knowing
bones should never grow like this. She said,
You become used to pain with time.

Now, an arterial leak thin as a newborn fingerling
flails past old urgencies, the oldest calcified by
years of settling. She's dying, her tallow skin
undermined by the wick burning down. The body,
a thought letting go. I sit beside her bed wandering
my rooms. She wanders hers. The pink hollyhocks
outside the bedroom window sigh at the weight
of the walls, and white chenille from the bedspread
drifts into piles. Embroidered cushions multiply like mice.

My thin words want to tie her to the sunshine yellow
naugahyde chairs in the kitchen, but they're growing legs
and running down the hall; wrap her in the baby-blue drapes
flying out the window like birds; hold her with arms
grown too heavy and large to lift, but she's gone,
except her eyes. The left iris
exploded by some inexplicable light, the other
looking somewhere behind me with such surprise,
I want to fall into its blue seeing.

LIGHT DESCENDS

Light has the quality of falling.
I know this. I saw it in my father's face,
the way light fell on it, softened it
into something indefinable —
like the taste of a Communion wafer
melting on the tongue, the acidic red
of the wine after, the careful turn
of the goblet, shared and wiped clean
with a white linen napkin.

The new dock goes nowhere, but leads somewhere,
an isthmus of planks, a place to stand,
its pilings driven down to bedrock and
tarred against rot. He stands on the shore and
shades his eyes to judge the certainty of lines and angles,
the singularity of this pointing. The beach
is deserted, but the repetitive boom of the pile driver
stays with him, a sound that measures distance
between itself and near or far, adjusts
repeatedly. He notices the conveyance of that pounding
from the right side of his heart to his lungs,
short and wide and venous, and
breathes it out through his mouth,
a sideways drowning. The ocean
crests in standing waves, points of resonance,
collects sound and shapes it
into whatever it wishes — trills and clicks, shushings,
themes sung by creatures so old men have forgotten
how they were swallowed whole and released
to walk home on planks of water — singing.

THE BRANCH THAT HOLDS US

An eagle falls without knowing its falling,
what up or down is. It flies the thin water of sky
like a pour of grace, breaks the properties of air
into flexion and extension, wide, bold wing strokes.
Time is a hunger, a slanted eye, open or closed,
light or dark, the past and future out of sight.

Only we know the hooked branch that grafts the past
to now, the weight of wood and skull,
the thin rings of dry years. We sit and watch,
our eyes frozen open like a horned owl's,
pare the moon sliver by sliver until there is just light
enough to see the distance we've fallen.

But there have been times when I imagined myself
a bird suspended in the moment, and
trusted barbs and barbules would hold,
saw how the corn flowers I picked so long ago
were the most precious blue, the sky fallen to bits, and
I knew how small everything is, how perfect.

COGNAC

The sweet clarity of cognac poured in the evening,
the round belly of the glass warmed in my hands,

earth squeezed and concentrated into this, time
spent together in front of a good fire. Recollections:

my mother gathering amber on the beaches of the Baltic,
wearing it around her throat. She magnetized it

into where we came from, insects caught
in the underwater twilight of a land drowning itself.

After she came to Canada, she never looked back,
swam a dry prairie sea, left the irreconcilable

in a sheet camp in Berlin: faceted water,
cut and strung into a dwindling continuum,

said she didn't want to choke herself with the past
anymore. She taught me to be fully awake, to taste

cognac, the fire of grapes ageing into themselves,
the insistence of slowness, the immediacy of heat.

I tell you, life has been rich. I have known time
to stand still, light to stay suspended in a bead of amber,

and with it has come a surety, a belief love satiates us
enough to face our hunger, the acceleration of gravity,

the long winter. Don't say anything. Tonight I believe
in immortality, that we will live longer than desire

and know one another; be smoothed and filled
by the earth itself.

If you dig in the earth here,
you'll know it as ocean bed,
sand mixed with water memory and
man memory, mixed with tides,
columns of rain, columns of fire;
photographs and kitchen implements
lying side by side with Rosenthal china
and white clam shell like demi-tasse,
amber like yellow Bleikrystal.
You'll know it as home,
the clay of your ancestors,
their flesh, their fine bones
laid down in strata

Karl Wiehler (1945) fell in Southern France

Johann Wiehler (1945) died in Dirschau while fleeing

Alfred Wiehler (1945) fell in Hungary

Gerhard Wiehler (1945) captured by Russians, never seen again

Fritz Wiehler (1945) captured by Russians, never seen again

Herbert Wiehler (1945) captured by Russians, never seen again

Marie Wiehler (1945) died in Nogat while fleeing

Gunther Wiehler (1945) missing in action on Russian Front

Herzleide Wiehler (1945) died in unknown location while fleeing

Christel Wiehler (1945) lost in sinking of Goya with her two children

Anna Wiehler (1945)   lost in sinking of Goya

Erika Wiehler (1945) lost in sinking of Goya

Marie Wiehler (1945) lost in sinking of Goya

Marian Wiehler (1945) lost in sinking of Goya

Liesbeth Wiehler (1945) disappeared en route to Denmark

Rudolf Wiehler (1945) died on Russian Front